Illusion and Reality
The cooperative idea: a constant companion throughout the history of mankind.

Germany sees its cooperative system as being at the heart of the international cooperative movement. It even actually believes that Delitzsch, Flammersfeld and Weyerbusch, the towns associated with Hermann Schulze-Delitzsch and Friedrich Wilhelm Raiffeisen, are the birthplaces of the cooperative idea. Such claims are completely unfounded, as Kaltenborn proves with the aid of a wealth of documents. The idea and practice of cooperatives have always existed throughout the evolution and history of mankind. Neanderthal man already demonstrated cooperative behaviour when hunting big game, and cooperatives actually existed in a variety of different forms in Europe during ancient history and the Middle Ages, a fact well-known to Schulze-Delitzsch.

The beginning of the modern era marked a growing rise in literary and theoretical interest in the cooperative idea in Europe. Its practical application took on a wide variety of forms. This development culminated with the founding of a consumer cooperative by the "Rochdale Society of Equitable Pioneers" in the English town of Rochdale in 1844. The principles defined by this society are still those of the International Co-operative Alliance today.

Schulze-Delitzsch and Raiffeisen each formed their own cooperative concept shortly afterwards, based on the ideas in discussion and practice at that time. Both also pursued much wider socio-political goals, of which cooperative interaction was just one element.

Germany has now requested that the cooperative idea be declared intangible cultural heritage of humanity by UNESCO in Paris. There could be no objection to this if it were not for the false justification that the cooperative idea was of German inspiration and first implemented by Schulze-Delitzsch and Raiffeisen. The cooperative idea is in fact a universal idea – and therefore ultimately naturally belongs to the intangible cultural heritage of humanity, without the need for any UNESCO declaration.

Martin Bergner

This book is dedicated to all those,
known and unknown,
who have developed and participated
in cooperative human interaction
around the world over the centuries.

Wilhelm Kaltenborn

Illusion and Reality

The cooperative idea:
a constant companion throughout the
history of mankind.

Published by Zentralkonsum eG
Neue Grünstraße 18, 10179 Berlin, Tel.: 030-27584-0
www.zentralkonsum.de

cover: © akg-images / Johann Brandstetter
Translation: Joanna Langworthy-Durier
Editing: Uta G. Barth

Manufactured and published by:
Books on Demand GmbH, Norderstedt 2016

ISBN: 978-3-842-36632-9

Contents

The issue in question

In spring 2015, the German Commission for UNESCO nominated the "cooperative idea" for inclusion in the Representative List of the Intangible Cultural Heritage of Humanity at UNESCO headquarters in Paris (see German UNESCO 2015a). It has already figured in the German inventory of intangible cultural heritage since 2014, alongside the Rhineland Carnival, the Pied Piper of Hamelin, German bread culture and other mostly regional customs and traditions. So why not the cooperative idea? Why should it not be declared cultural heritage of humanity? So let us look at the reasons why it should. What does the cooperative idea actually mean and where it does come from? The German Commission for UNESCO offers a justification for its nomination. This includes the very serious claim that the idea and practice of cooperatives spread from Delitzsch, Weyerbusch and Flammersfeld (where German cooperative founders Hermann Schulze-Delitzsch and Friedrich Wilhelm Raiffeisen began their work) "to other parts of Germany and beyond. Today it is practiced nearly worldwide." (German UNESCO 2015a).

This is simply inaccurate and untrue, and the claim is reason enough to examine the matter in more detail: how did the idea and practice of cooperatives actually develop? This is what the following pages aim to answer, in an unavoidably abridged manner. The most important findings are listed in the summary.

In the nomination by the German Commission for UNESCO, the German word "Genossenschaftsidee" (cooperative idea) was translated into English as "the idea and practice of organizing shared interests in cooperatives" (see German UNESCO 2015b). Let us start with the actual idea. It was none other than Hermann Schulze-Delitzsch who labelled the idea of the cooperative, of cooperation, as the "association of separate small individual forcesin the interest of common aims[1]" (Schulze-Delitzsch 1858: 68). This definition in fact covers all forms of human

1 *Vereinigung atomistisch vereinzelter kleiner Kräfte zur Erreichung gemeinschaftlicher Zwecke*

cooperation, all of which could be given the name cooperative, and does not just concern economic goals. Indeed, Schulze-Delitzsch also called the workers' educational associations that he initiated and sponsored 'cooperatives', regardless of their legal form.

The cooperative idea is a universal idea

Another important cooperative figure, this time from our century, can also be quoted: Ivano Barberini, President of the International Co-operative Alliance from 2001 until his death in 2009, declared that the cooperative idea is in man's DNA; traces can be found in the experiences of each and every one of us. Every generation of children is told the tale of prehistoric man, who, once he began to hunt, fish and cultivate the ground, quickly learnt that better results could be achieved by working together, cooperating. (see Barberini 2009: 16/17). Finally, in more modern times "generations of philosophers, politicians, religious leaders and cooperative members [...] elaborated the idea of the cooperative according to their personal convictions." (Barberini 2009: 42). In other words, the cooperative idea is a universal idea.

A German cooperative theorist, Richard Sigmund Schultze, laconically declared, as early as 1867, that "the history of mankind is also the history of association". (Schultze 1867: 5). Another more recent author, the rather conservative legal historian Bernd-Rüdiger Kern is just as succinct: "The very first and most important form of human association to date is the cooperative". (Kern 1998: 82). The prestigious University of Michigan in Ann Arbor declares in an online publication under the heading "The Cooperative Movement" that "people learned ages ago that by working together they can accomplish more than the sum of each individual's efforts. [...] The history of human economic cooperation is perhaps older than the history of competition" (see University of Michigan 2015).

German economist and cooperative theorist Willy Wygodzinsiki made a similar statement a century ago: "Cooperative formations can be found as far back as we can see in the history of human activity; yes, we can truly say that the cooperative economy is at the origin of economic history, and that individual economic units are only a later form." (Wygodzinski 1911: 6).

Anthropological findings on cooperatives

These clear statements are supported by scientific anthropology, for example by the following somewhat lengthy observation: "People are the uncontested world champions in cooperation. [...] In experiments, so-called 'public goods games', subjects distribute their own goods fairly, in other words to their own disadvantage, and without obtaining any visible advantage from this altruistic act. They even go one step further and punish fellow players for uncooperative behaviour, even if this punishment is at their own cost. [...] Human behaviour evolved in situations of strong competition between neighbouring groups. In such situations, it can be more advantageous to the group if it is composed of cooperative members." Cooperation seems to be based on reciprocity, in that help given to someone today will be reciprocated by him or a third-party tomorrow.(Ostner 2009: 240/241). Another identical observation just phrases it differently: "Cooperation is based on empathetic identification: it is necessary to participate in the aims of another to achieve effective cooperation; the aim of another becomes one's own concern." (Bischof-Köhler 2009: 315). Two anthropologists vividly declare in a joint article that "The horrors of reality" can be "considerably reduced by understanding and cooperation, particularly within a social community" (Großheim 2009: 214). The horrors of reality were alleviated by consumer cooperatives more often than we would like to imagine and it is not without reason that they were known as "Kinder der Not[2] " during the 19th century.

2 *Children of distress*

The earliest statements of anthropological relevance, which were of philosophical rather than actual scientific substance, also made similar observations. This was the case of Plato, whose view can be summarised in a modern interpretation as follows: each of us is inadequate alone and requires others. Man is therefore apparently dependent on the help of his fellow men, on cooperative relations (see Jörke 2009: 442/443). Aristotle also saw man as a social being in need of cooperative relations (see Jörke 2009: 444). This is the famous definition of man as a "zoon politikon", to which Aristotle adds that he who is unable to live in society, or who has no need because he is sufficient for himself, must be either a beast or a god (see Aristotle 1971: 65ff.), and is therefore beyond human spheres.

Cooperation in prehistoric times

Man's ability to cooperate, or rather his need to do so, is visible from research on prehistory. The Homo habilis, founder of the Oldowan culture, lived in East Africa around two million years ago. It is very probable, according to Stone Age researcher, Hansjürgen Müller-Beck, that "social contact within groups and sexes [...] also gradually intensified and evolved over generations" as a result of this developing division of labour. (Müller-Beck 2004: 40/41).

Around 1.6 million years later, Homo erectus, the species of man that lived at that time, had spread to Europe. Bone remains found at the Bilzingsleben Palaeolithic site in the north of Thuringia in Germany allow us to conclude that Homo erectus hunted big game. "As it is difficult to imagine that a forest elephant could be tracked and killed by just one hunter alone, it is possible to draw conclusions on the social behaviour of early man. Homo erectus hunted this type of game in groups, and the participants also needed a system of communication to agree on their individual tasks." (Terberger 2002: 66).

Homo erectus became extinct and was replaced by the Neanderthal, Homo neanderthalensis, in Europe 200,000 years ago. Almut Bick describes a hunting scene from that time: "The herd of wild horses is visible from afar. It slowly approaches the watering place on the lake shore. The hunters remain hidden, letting them come to a distance of 10, 20m. Wooden spears then hail down upon the animals. The herd flees but a good dozen have been hit. The men dismember their prey there and then, and store it. They are pleased: the meat and hides will see their family through the winter. This type of hunting scene took place in Schöningen, Lower Saxony, in the early Middle Palaeolithic period." Neanderthals also took their chance against big game. "It would take a group of hunters to defeat big game, not just one man." (Bick 2012: 61ff.).

Homo sapiens later prevailed. "Homo sapiens is primarily a social animal. Social cooperation is our key for survival and reproduction. It is not enough for individual men and women to know the whereabouts of lions and bison. It is much more important for them to know who in their band hates whom, who is sleeping with whom, who is honest and who is a cheat". It was then possible to spread this information - around 70,000 years ago - thanks to Homo sapien's newly-acquired linguistic abilities. "Reliable information about who could be trusted meant that small bands could expand into larger bands, and Sapiens could develop tighter and more sophisticated types of cooperation." (Harari 2015: 35/36).

The oldest Neolithic town, Catal Hüyük in the highlands of southern Anatolia, existed 9,000 years ago. One of the buildings has been identified as a hunting shrine. Its walls are covered with paintings. The antechamber "depicts a group of men attacking a herd of deer. Two hunters have already slain one the animals. The wall painting in the main chamber shows a giant bull, circled by tiny men armed with bows and dressed in leopard skin loincloths." (Bick 2012: 102ff.). Cooperative hunting therefore continued, even amongst Homo sapiens.

Around 5,000 years ago, at the end of the so-called Linear Pottery culture, Central Europe saw the development of "centralised sites with a higher population. People grew closer together in everyday life during these difficult times. During the age of Linear Pottery culture, each of the huge longhouses housed only one family. In the Middle Neolithic period, however, several families often shared one roof. The houses which were up to 50 m in length now had partition walls, separating off chambers for individual families. The community structure changed. There is now the first evidence of community buildings and shared facilities. Each family no longer collected the clay used to seal house walls from its own pit, but used the communal pit at the edge of the village". (Bick 2012: 122). This was a very early form of raw material association. "The up to 100 m² large open porches at the south-east end then served as a community/work room. Middle Neolithic society displayed a much stronger, integrating community structure in these living conditions than was evident during the age of Linear Pottery culture". (Lüning 2002: 127).

What had obviously always existed since the origin of man, whatever the species, was the "association of separate small individual forces in the interest of common aims", which Schulze-Delitzsch saw as the implementation of the cooperative idea, the idea of cooperation. It is part of being human – in the same way as humans care for their offspring. Man would not be here today without millions of years of maternal instinct. So should raising children also be declared intangible cultural heritage of humanity? On the subject of raising children: anyone who has had the pleasure of observing children in a playground, does not need to be an expert in anthropology and prehistory to comprehend that cooperative behaviour is a natural human trait, just as much as conflict. Barberini knew this. However, despite all these findings, the German Commission for UNESCO defies common sense, believing itself capable of pinpointing the exact geographical location in which the idea and practice of organizing shared interests in cooperatives began.

Cooperatives in written history

The second task would now be to examine where and how cooperative activities occurred in written history and in what form. This has to be limited to Europe for several reasons. Two publications are a major source of help here: one is the "Internationales Handwörterbuch des Genossenschaftswesens[3]", published by Vahan Totomianz in 1928, in which around 140 authors discuss more than 530 terms from the world and history of cooperatives. This concise dictionary is a true cooperative encyclopaedia. The second is the online "Centro italiano di documentazione sulle cooperazione e l'economia sociale[4]", which provides an overview of the history and principles of the cooperative system, focussing essentially on Italy, but with sufficient international outlook. Its brief summary of cooperative history begins in 1750. There is currently nothing comparable in German. So what can we learn from this dictionary and online publication, and other histories of cooperatives?

Cooperatives in ancient history

Hans Müller, General Secretary of the International Co-operative Alliance from 1908 to 1913, dealt with the terms relating to Classical Antiquity in the dictionary of 1928 and came to the clear conclusion that "the question of whether cooperatives or cooperative-like formations existed during the period of ancient history [...] can be answered with an unconditional yes." (Müller 1928a: p. 22).

With regard to the situation in Ancient Greece, he explains that "Almost every member of the Greek middle and lower classes belonged to a cooperative, which guaranteed its members a burial place and a decent burial, and also promoted social contact and mutual assistance. ... From these religious-social cultural

3 *International Dictionary and the Cooperative System*
4 *Italian Documentation Centre on Cooperatives and Social Economy*

cooperatives [...] then grew those with primarily professional and economic aims. Some of these cooperatives operated a common purchasing system for fuels and beverages. Others provided assistance for the poor or for members in temporary need; others obliged their members to offer one another board and lodging when travelling. Many even combined of all these aims and more. Members of these cooperatives were not just free men and citizens, but also slaves, foreigners, and even women, suggesting a free and guaranteed right of association. Cooperative matters were settled by members themselves, generally during the usual monthly general meetings, which formed the highest authority. [...] An annual general meeting was commonly held in the spring, accompanied by a festive meal." (Müller 1928a: 6). This paints a surprisingly modern picture characterised by self-help, voluntary action, self-management and general meetings as the highest authority.

In an "award-winning essay" from 1909, the author speaks of the wealth of material available on the Greek cooperative system (see Poland 1909: 19). He also sees cooperatives as entirely natural phenomenon amongst men. Cooperatives of merchants, tradesmen, athletes, artists etc. "are mostly small groups of individuals that naturally come together wherever people live in communities [...]" (Poland 1909: 4). A contemporary of that era is also called on as a witness: Plato records in one of his letters that the ruler of Syracuse, the Greek colony on the island of Sicily, returned home accompanied by two brothers from Athens, "a friendship whose origin did not lie in philosophy but in the cooperative system in vogue [...]." (Plato 1921: 60).

Hans Müller writes of Ancient Rome that the "cooperative trade associations called collegia" probably originated from "religious cooperatives" (see Müller 1928a: 7). An expert historian, Karl-Wilhelm Weber, explains that "Membership was voluntary. Efforts were no doubt also made to promote professional interests amongst the general public. The most important aspect was, however, the social function of these associations. Members usually got together once a month in the association's own meeting place (schola); poorer cooperative groups met in taverns. [...] Professional associations frequently included burial funds, guaranteeing members a burial place and a 'fitting' memorial in return for a single or regular payment." (Weber 1995: 169/170).

An older description is even more specific: a collegium is the "name for an association of people with a common, lasting goal". A collegium requires a minimum of three people (as in the German Cooperative Societies Act (Genossenschaftsgesetz) today). Private collegia included "associations of professional colleagues of any kind". They "also reflected the efforts of the weaker and poorer to become stronger through association and to have more influence than would have been possible alone". "Freedom of association" existed during the time of the Republic. "The internal autonomy of the collegia was based on their statutes." Even "dissolution of an association was in general voluntary [...]". There were also collegia for women of the same profession. Slaves too were entitled to membership. Different collegia counted between 16 and 1,500 members. Decisions were made and elections held during the general meeting (Kornemann 1901: 380ff.). The classical definition of cooperatives was therefore also put into practice in Ancient Rome: the weaker become stronger by association.

The cooperative also has a very long history in Germany. "We come across cooperatives in the first Germanic tribes. Cooperatives shaped their national life and gave structure to the whole community. They could be found in narrow and wider circles, in public and private relations, as the element connecting social and state organisation. The Gau[5] coooperative and Mark[6] cooperative belonged to the tribe cooperative, and while the Volksgemeinde[7], the Gau cooperative's decision-making body, made decisions on issues such as war and peace and the tribe's most important interests in open meetings, the 'Thing' (cooperative assembly) administered [...] justice [...]. Märker,

5 *Discrid cooperative*
6 *Joint territory cooperative*
7 *People's community*

cooperative members who owned a Feldmark (arable land), determined matters relating to land, particularly communal ownership of woods and pastures etc. Finally, battle cooperatives were formed under elected leaders for war and looting campaigns. Indeed, a number of tribes even temporarily joined together in this type of federation in the face of common danger or for the purpose of a large, joint venture." This observation was made by none other than Schulze-Delitzsch (Schulze-Delitzsch 1865: 223/224) and he even goes so far as to claim that the victory in the Teutoburg Forest over two thousand years ago was that of the German cooperative: "Roman power was, for example, smashed in the Teutoburg Forest thanks to this type of association of Germanic tribes." (Schulze-Delitzsch 1865: 224).

Schulze-Delitzsch, astonishingly, goes even further when he says "The characteristic features of cooperative associations at that time were essentially the same as those that can be observed in our cooperatives today, despite the change in tasks. [...] The highest level of self-determination and self-management with the direct participation of all cooperative members when managing common matters formed the culminating features that we still adhere to in our cooperative societies and economic cooperatives today." (Schulze-Delitzsch 1865: 224). In other words, Schulze-Delitzsch clearly contradicts the German Commission for UNESCO, as in his view, it all started in the ancient forests of Germania, not in Delitzsch.

Cooperatives in the Middle Ages

Certain cooperative associations in Russia date back to the Middle Ages. "Associations, of a form similar to Italian work cooperatives, could be found long before any influence from the western cooperative movement. First carpenters, then masons, then fishermen, shortly followed by transport tradesmen and workers, joined together to perform common tasks, either for their own account or for that of an employer to whom they jointly sold their work. Farmers working their own land also joined together to prevent being exploited by intermediaries. These associations are known under the name 'Artel' and their origins date back to the Middle Ages. They were the most common form of Russian cooperative until the end of the XIXth century." (Totomianz 1928a: 765; see also Ulitin 1928: 39ff.).

Cooperative models played an extremely important role in European agriculture during the Middle Ages. This was the case with the implementation of the three-field system in the High Middle Ages, in the tenth and eleventh century.   Rural land was used for a different purpose every year for three years: summer crops, winter crops and fallow land, after which the whole process was repeated. This was so-called crop rotation. It protected the soil and increased crop yield, which was urgently needed in view of the growing population. Forest clearance accelerated to extend arable land during the eleventh and twelfth century.   The landlords offered "protection and organisation, but the farmers or farming cooperative bore the brunt of the work. [...]." (see Dettelbacher 1988: 234). Bernd-Rüdiger Kern is even more explicit when he observes that the three-field system would have been inconceivable without the cooperative. (see Kern 1998: 83).

This was particularly true for Zelgensysteme[8]. These were systems of land use "in which the fields of a settlement were divided into large areas, so-called Zelgen. Each Zelge was made up of strips of land belonging to many different owners and was planted with the same crop. As the individual holdings were not accessible by paths, the villagers had to cooperate in the communal management of the fields. [...] The crop rotation system was managed identically in village fields when it came to planting cycles and type of crop, due to binding agreements." (Schnyder 2015). "The village cooperative or village leader decides when crops are to be sown and harvested, when the sown field is to be fenced or when the fence is to be removed so that it can be used as a stubble field by village cattle after the harvest." (Rösener 1985: 55).

8   Open field systems

The 13th and 14th century saw the development of "substantial free farming communities [...] Inspired by the flourish of urban municipalities, the communal movement also spread in rural areas and contributed to the development of territorial farming cooperatives both in the south of the German Empire and in districts along the North Sea coast. [...] In coastal areas, flood defences, dyke construction and the communal organisation of land improvement positively encouraged the formation of farming cooperatives." (Rösener: 1985: 237/238).

Common land should be mentioned in this context. It "is used collectively by all the village farmers: common grazing land is shared by cattle and the woodland is available for use by all farmers resident in the village." (Rösener 1985: 56). During the High Middle Ages, the region between the rivers Harz, Elbe and Saale, which was "predominantly defined by Old Saxon constitutional elements", saw the development of a village commune led by a Bauermeister (master farmer), "very similar to the village cooperative". "They not only had common land, but also streets and paths, bake houses, parish halls, taverns and sometimes mills." (Rösener 1985: 175).

Historical forms of cooperatives in Germany – past and present

Other areas of German society – and this was not the only country concerned – were given a cooperative structure during the Middle Ages. With the advent of the Early Modern Period came new cooperative structures. One such example were the Hauberg cooperatives in Siegerland. Hauberg is the German term for coppices of hardwood, mainly oak trees, on mountain slopes. These Hauberge supplied a fourfold yield due to rotating use: oak bark for tanneries, wood (originally for charcoal, later for heating purposes), arable land and grazing pastures. Use followed on a cooperative basis. Each associate was allocated a share of the Hauberg. Work was then carried out at the same time, but not

19

collectively, by the individual users. Shares could differ in size. The Hauberg was closed for several years in one specific cycle, so that the wood could grow back. During this time, the shares of the Hauberg cooperative members were returned to the cooperative. Shares were then reallocated, in a completely different manner at the start of the next period of use. (See Delius 1909: 5ff.). The Hauberg cooperatives developed in this form during the first half of the 15th century. Until then, "uncontrolled forestry in cooperative coppices had led to forest destruction, which was worrying at a time when the flourishing Siegerland iron industry began to demand more and more wood (charcoal) [...]." This is how established procedures developed for the cooperative use of coppices. (Delius 1909: 36).

Today's existing forms of Hauberg cooperatives and other types of forestry cooperatives in North Rhine Westphalia are based on a single federal state law, the Community Forest Act (Gemeinschaftswaldgesetz) of April 1975, the second section of which lists the regulations for a forest cooperative (see Gemeinschaftswaldgesetz 2015: §§ 9ff.). The Community Forest Act in North Rhine Westphalia and also in Thuringia also stipulates the procedure for founding new forest cooperatives (see Gemeinschaftswaldgesetz 2015: §§ 39ff.; Thüringer Waldgesetz 2015: § 52). Germany, therefore, does not just have a single law on cooperatives.

Traditional and lost forms of cooperative organisation from the Middle Ages and Early Modern Period were not just a source of interest to Schulze-Delitzsch during the 19th century. They also inspired many members of the legal profession. One of the leading jurists in this movement was Georg Karl Christoph Beseler, born a year after Schulze-Delitzsch. A succinct description of him states that "His biggest economic achievement is the development of the cooperative theory [...]." Beseler "described the associative spirit of the German nation as being a distinctive characteristic of Germanic law" and gave "the corporative cooperative, the German legal entity, its essential doctrinal justification." (Lang-Hinrichsen 1955: 174/175).

20

Beseler's major work bore the title "System des gemeinen deutschen Privatrechts[9]" and was published in two volumes in 1885. His use of the collective term "corporative cooperative" covered the upper aristocracy's family cooperative, the Markgenossenschaft, the water and pasture cooperatives of land owners, the dyke association, as well as tradesmen associations including guilds, joint-stock companies, insurance associations and widows' funds, bank and credit associations and finally "associations with religious, artistic, scientific and social aims, so-called Erholungsgesellschaften[10] etc." (see Beseler 1885: 286/287).

Beseler also wrote "The associative movement, i.e. the association of several individuals to achieve the same goal through shared efforts and means, has not developed as vigorously in any other area of German life as in trade business circles. From the mere temporary closed consortium for individual commercial transactions to the corporative cooperative of the joint-stock company, we have seen the development of a wide variety of singular organisations [...]." (Beseler 1885: 1034). Beseler's definition of an association or cooperative as "the association of several individuals to achieve the same goal through shared efforts and means" is virtually congruent with Schulze-Delitzsch's "association of separate small individual forces in the interest of common aims" – and both were aware that the underlying idea is age-old.

Another important jurist, who followed in Beseler's footsteps by devoting himself to traditional forms of German law, is still well-known today: Otto Friedrich von Gierke, born in 1841. Inspired by Beseler, Gierke's post-doctoral thesis dealt with "the research field to which he was to remain faithful until the end of his days: the history and law of the German cooperative." His life's work was dedicated to the legal understanding "of cooperative and corporate law in particular". For Gierke, the "traditional basic concept of the Germanic cooperative" was the benchmark "for

9 System of German Common Private Law
10 Recreation societies

correct law" (see Wolf 1963: 675). Gierke also saw the more recent joint-stock companies of his time as cooperatives. He even declared that "after several aborted preliminary attempts, the capital cooperative has achieved perfection in the joint-stock company." (Gierke 1881: 911). To quote the German Wikipedia site for once, Gierke is also "known as 'the father of cooperative law' due to his many decisive contributions.[11]" (see Wikipedia 2015).

Three centuries of cooperative history in modern times: The beginning

There was a troupe of Italian actors in the 16th century which can confidently be compared with a modern-day cooperative. At the beginning of 1545, a troupe of 8 professional actors concluded a contract in Padua, recorded in a notarial document. The participants formed a "fraternal society" ("far una fraternel compagnia"), which was to last – from Easter 1545 – until carnival in 1546 (three members of this troupe then founded a new "compagnia" with other actors in Venice in April 1546). It was a travelling troupe of Commedia dell'Arte. A horse therefore had to be purchased to transport their effects (props and costumes) from town to town. The contract made provisions for mutual equal rights. The leader ("capo") was elected (this was a certain Ser Maphio, known as Zanini of Padua). He was elected before the notarisation. All takings were to go to the fellowship. The money was to be stored in a chest ("cassella") to which three members of the troupe would have the key. All expenses, such as the purchase and upkeep of the horse, travel costs and any possible medical costs, were to be paid from this chest. The remaining proceeds would then be shared out equally ("divisi egualmente") between the eight members of the troupe at the end." (see Cocco 1915: 55ff.; Venturini 2011; see also Mehnert 2003: 12/13 for a short note in German).

11 *Wegen seiner entscheidenden Beiträge zum Genossenschaftsrecht gilt er als*
  "Vater des Genossenschaftsrecht"

This is a temporary cooperative (which the German Cooperative Societies Act still recognises today). Membership was voluntary. The leader was elected. The cooperative served for the purpose of its members' purchases. The economic profit was shared out equally. Very few decisions can have been made on the comedies to be played and the distribution of roles which is why such terms were not necessary in the contract. The Commedia dell'Arte was well-known for having fixed roles and using much improvisation (see Mehnert 2003: passim). Schulze-Delitzsch would not have had any trouble including this troupe in his "Allgemeinen Verband der auf Selbsthilfe beruhenden deutschen Erwerbs- und Wirtschaftsgenossenschaften[12]". There are no doubt many more such examples gathering dust in the archives, amongst the documents of 16th century notary publics – particularly in Northern Italy.

Chronology of further developments in cooperative history

Over the course of history, examples of cooperative associations and theoretical and literary contemplations on the topic became more and more frequent. They are listed below in chronological order.

1654 – 1725 are the dates of birth and death of John Bellers, "who was the first recorded person to develop and recommend cooperative thought as a practical means of transforming the way the existing economy functioned." (Müller 1928b: 84). The publication in which he developed his basic philosophy is entitled "Proposals for Raising a Colledge of Industry of all useful Trades and Husbandry [...]". As Eduard Bernstein wrote in his work on the great English Revolution, this "Colledge" was to be understood as a "labour colony or cooperative." (see Bernstein 1922: 331/332).

---

12 *General Association of German Purchasing and Trading Cooperatives based on self-help*

1715 A certain Parson Jordan founded a "mutual insurance society against livestock disease" in Pabjanice/Lodz, Poland (Zawada 1928: 693).

1740 – 1826 are the dates of birth and death of Johann Friedrich Oberlins, who "is viewed as one of the earliest instigators of cooperative principles on the continent." (Röhrken 1928: 662). He was a parson in Waldersbach on the border between Lorraine and Alsace, an area of infinite and above all rural poverty. Oberlin endeavoured to provide help in a variety of different forms. In the 1770s, he founded a "Société agricole". This society was part of a regional network of mutual help, which had developed gradually over time in an effort to fight misery. "Farmers take their fate into their own hands as time goes by; they switch to new methods [of agricultural production], and the Société agricole becomes an extended arm of the agricultural reforms initiated by Oberlin." (Chalmel 2012: 150).

1750 Cheesemakers' cooperatives were founded in Franche-Comté. These were the first producer cooperatives. (see Centro italiano 2015).

In the same year, Benjamin Franklin founded a cooperative-style insurance society (which still exists today under a different name) in Philadelphia (see Centro italiano 2015).

1758 The first American agricultural cooperative society was founded in Philadelphia (see Centro italiano 2015).

1761 The Fenwick Weaver's Society was founded in Fenwick/Scotland. It originally aimed to promote technical standards amongst members. It later became a consumer cooperative. The International Co-operative Alliance describes it as the first real cooperative. (see ICA 2013).

During the 1870s, Carl Gottlieb Svarez (or Suarez), a young jurist working for the Prussian states was given the task of creating an agricultural credit system for the province of Silesia.

In his eyes, "a cooperative-style bond institute was to be established, which could lend its members, the landowners, up to half the value of their estates in cash in exchange for mortgages. This cooperative, called 'Landschaft' was to use the acquired mortgages as bonds, for which it acted as guarantor, for securities trading. The interest rate of these bonds was guaranteed by the 'Landschaft´." The new credit system quickly became established. "It later contributed to an improvement in the economic situation of the Silesian aristocracy." (Wolf 1963: 434/434). These cooperative "Landschaften" also developed in the provinces of East and West Prussia. Membership was compulsory in many cases (see Weber 1998: 333ff.).

1780 The first cooperative in Greece was established in Ambelakia (see Centro italiano 2015).

1781 The novel "Leonard and Gertrude" by Heinrich Pestalozzi, depicting the cooperative ideal, was published in Switzerland. In the story's happy ending, the villagers pay "one and a half Kreuzer" to a "tax fund" for each sheaf cut over 25 years to liquidate all taxes and duties to the manor that clung to their land. (see Pestalozzi 1933: 214ff.).

1786 The following was reported: "Matters, for which there is still inadequate provision to date in civil society, undoubtedly include death in those middle-class families, which are neither rich nor poor, but have a meagre income. The illness of one its members is quickly the cause of financial setback in such households: and should death follow, the extortionate burial costs in some places are often harder to bear than the loss of the person alone. [...] Private citizens therefore had the idea of easing the burden by sharing it amicably amongst themselves. Corpse and death funds, mourning cooperatives and other such societies have therefore been established, which, upon the death of one of their members, pay out a certain sum to the dead member's heirs, raised by equal contributions." (Becker 1786: 4ff.).

1794 Watchmaker's cooperatives were established in Vienna (see Centro italiano 2015).

1799 "Les Phalanstères", cooperative communities based on principles of voluntarism, harmony and self-support, were founded in France by Charles Fourier (see Centro italiano 2015).

1806 The first modern dairy cooperative was established in Osoppo, Italy (see Centro italiano 2015).

1809 Gardeners' and farmers' associations established the very first cooperatives in Luxembourg (see Centro italiano 2015).

1812 The Friendly Victualling Society was founded in Lennoxtown, Scotland, the first cooperative with a refund system (see Hasselmann 1971: 14). It still existed in 1912, just like the cooperatives founded in Meltham Mill in 1827, in Bannockburn in 1830, in Hanley and in Ripponden in 1832, in Arbroath in 1833, in West Port in 1834, in East Wemyss in 1837, in Leslie in 1839, in Darvel, in S. Crosland and in Tillicoultry in 1840, in Freuchie in 1842, in Kettle and in Falkland in 1843, in Alva, in Hepworth, in Crewe and in Anchtermuchty in 1845, in Todmorden, in Selkirk, in Dysart and in Montrose in 1846, in Barrowford, in Leeds, in Dumfries and in Menstrie in 1847 (see Cole 1944: Map "The Spread of Cooperation").

1816 An agricultural cooperative was established in Hrubieszow, Russian-controlled Poland at that time (see Centro italiano 2015).

Cheesemakers' cooperative societies were founded in Bern and Fribourg, Switzerland in the same year. These were the very first Swiss cooperatives (see Centro italiano 2015).

A weavers' producer cooperative, "The Liberties", was established in Dublin (see Kulemann 1922: 141).

1817 Heinrich Zschokke's political novel "Das Goldmacherdorf[13]" was published in Switzerland, portraying the theory of cooperative self-help. The Federation of Swiss Consumer Associations published a commented edition in its series "Pioniere und Theoretiker des Genossenschaftswesens[14]". The annotations included an observation on the village education system in Zschokke's novel "It is immediately obvious that [...] this system is also the clear pedagogic expression of the social principle of the consumer cooperative organisation." (Zschokke 1918: 149). Another annotation reads "Here the poet describes the essential condition for every cooperative economy, as he understood it." (Zschokke 1918: 159). It states with regard to another passage "What is suggested here and is subsequently developed, is a type of agricultural association that corresponds roughly with a modern dairy cooperative." (Zschokke 1918: 163). Another village initiative is described as follows "A basic principle of the Rochdale plan is anticipated here under different circumstances." (Zschokke 1918: 170). In 1928, an entry in the "Internationales Handwörterbuch des Genossenschaftswesens" states that several of Zschokke's economic principles could "still be applied to cooperative administrative activities today". (Faucherre 1928: 694).

1820 A second weavers' producer cooperative was founded in Dublin (see Kulemann 1922: 141).

1821 The "Cooperative and Economical Society" was set up in London, inspired by Robert Owen, and published the "Economist", the first newspaper to deal with cooperative ideas (see Centro italiano 2015). The society relied on membership contributions. It undertook to observe political and religious neutrality. Every member had a vote. Members elected a management committee. It was based on the principles of voluntarism and the rejection of capital aid (see Totomianz 1928b: 675ff.).

13 The Goldmakers´ village
14 Pioneers and Theorists of the Cooperative System

1823 The concept of a cooperative-style Vereinsbank[15] developed in Bavaria to "unlock" the capital market "for agriculture", (see von Aretin 1823: passim).

1825 A consumer cooperative was established in Siberia, the first cooperative in Russia (see Centro italiano 2015), aside from those forms stemming from the Middle Ages.

1827 William King founded a consumer association in Brighton (see Wolff 1928: 135ff.), the "Cooperative Trading Association". It had permanent and inalienable community funds (see Gide 1928: 134/135). King advocated the political and religious tolerance of cooperatives. The latter were not just the concern of certain classes: "The cooperative system benefits all classes of the population", however dissemination of knowledge and enlightenment was necessary as "the biggest obstacle in the path of the cooperative movement is the ignorance of the working classes". (Totomianz 1928c: 545ff.).

1828 William King established the cooperative newspaper "The Co-operator" (see Totomianz 1928c: 545ff.).

1829 Cooperatives in and around Brighton founded a wholesale centre in Sussex (see Totomianz 1928d: 148).

1830 The first cooperative factory in the UK was established in London (see Centro italiano 2015).

266 cooperatives already existed in England at this time and totalled 20,000 members (see Totomianz 1928e: 459).

In the **1830s**, wandering journeymen founded dining cooperatives in Switzerland (see Katzenstein 1928a: 22).

1831 The first British cooperative congress was held in Manchester. By 1835, Robert Owen had instigated seven national cooperative congresses (see Centro italiano 2015).

15 Association bank

The first workers' cooperative was established in France (see Centro italiano 2015).

"A cooperative boom" was recorded in France **between 1831 and 1850** (see Daudé-Bancel 1928: 264ff.).

1832 Philippe Buchez advocated bylaws for local cooperatives that were to include the principle of a perpetual and non-transferable reserve fund into which one fifth of profit should be paid. He explicitly emphasised the voluntary nature of membership. He also set up a cabinetmakers' producer cooperative in Paris which existed until 1873. (see Gide 1928: 135). Its statutes stated "The undersigned cabinetmakers join together in an association, as it is only lack of sufficient capital and not of will which forces them into submission to employers. The latter, whose only effort is to advance their capital, fully exploit workers by keeping a much greater share of the fruit of the work than is due to them in view of their efforts. Isolation is most detrimental to the interests of workers, forcing them to submit unconditionally to the demands of masters etc. The undersigned have therefore decided to revoke this submission and to unite in favour of collective production in order to acquire their own capital, so that they and all workers who join them in this association, are able to take on work independently, guarantee support in the event of temporary cessation of work, provide for the education and tuition of children and for the upkeep of orphans and the incapacitated; in other words, the capital to be accumulated is to be used to fulfil man's sacred duties, those of brotherly love and mutual support etc." (quoted in Schultze 1867: 11/12). Schulze-Delitzsch used similar wording in Germany twenty years later.

1833 Michel Derrion and Joseph Peynier founded the "True and Social Cooperative Store" in Lyon, the first district cooperative with numerous branches throughout France (see Daudé-Bancel 1928: 264/265).

1834 A cooperative for the construction and operation of a windmill was founded in Homberg am Rhein (see Schreiber 1928: 640/641).

1835 English legislation authorised the formation of a central cooperative society with branches all over the world (see Centro italiano 2015).

1838 The "General Association of Spanish Cattle Breeders" was established in Madrid; this was the first cooperative in Spain (see Centro italiano 2015).

1839 A - short-lived - cooperative bakery was founded in Paris (see Gaumont 1928: 681).

A savings cooperative was founded in Orizaba, Mexico; the first cooperative in the country (see Centro italiano 2015).

1840 Louis Blanc published "L'Organisation du travail" in France, defining the basic principles of the workers' cooperative movement. The producer cooperative was, in Blanc's view, "the supreme cooperative" for solving social issues. (see Totomianz 1928f: 119 /120). Blanc advocated an "economic revolution and the gradual, peaceful, smooth abolition of the proletariat" through the establishment of cooperatives both in industry and agriculture, with some government aid (see Blanc 1899: 151ff.). Schulze-Delitzsch later pursued similar goals, admittedly in different forms. However, he shared Blanc's view that the producer cooperative played the most important role when it came to solving social issues.

The 1840s saw "the beginnings of a workers' cooperative movement" in the Czech provinces of Austria (see Fiser 1928: 886).

1841 Giuseppe Mazzini published the first chapters of "I Doveri dell'Uomo" (The Duties of Man). Mazzini saw cooperative associations as "the safest means to emancipation". In 1842, he founded the General Workers' Association whose goals included "promotion and relief of cooperatives". Producer cooperatives were at the heart of his model. The fundamental requirement of a cooperative was self-help. "It should be a free and voluntary association among men, who know, esteem and love each other, not imposed by the force of governmental authority, to be administered by your own delegates, and from which you should be free to withdraw at your own discretion." Mazzini also aimed to solve social issues in this manner. He spoke against state support, even in the form of credits. The cooperative capital was always to be self-financed. Loans were to be granted by credit unions. Membership was to be open. (see Manfredi 1928: 618ff.). Mazzini's beliefs were based on several philosophical and religious principles. These included: the existence of God; the law of progress which can be fulfilled through the path to humanity and the association of free nations; the sacredness of duty; in social matters: the education and material improvement of the masses through association, extended to all fields of civilian life, in order to unite all the forces of general good. Mazzini also advocated special credit forms to enable workers' cooperatives to own their means of production. (see Scirocco 1993: 178ff.).

Mazzini also proclaimed "Amongst the essential elements of human life, such as Religion, Liberty and Association, there is also Property. [...] The remedy to your sufferings, you workers, is to be found in the union of capital and labour in the same hands. All the permanent causes of your poverty will be removed, [...] when every man shall be producer and consumer alike. [...] Association of labour, and division of the fruits of labour, or rather the profits resulting from the sale of its products, among producers in proportion to the amount and value of the work done by each, this is the social future we aim for. [...] Liberty to withdraw without doing harm to the association, indivisibility and perpetuity of the collective capital, equal remuneration for all, distribution according to the quantity and quality of the work, these are the general principles upon which you must found your association." Mazzini summarised this in the triad "Freedom, Education, Association". He also wrote "Though superior to every other being by virtue of your association with your fellows, you are when isolated inferior in strength to many animals, and weak and incapable of development and of a complete existence. [...] There exist aims and ends which do not embrace all citizens but only a certain number of them, and they must have the right to found a special association." (Pederzani-Weber 1888: 30ff.). "The right to association is sacred as it places the individual within the community with others." (Mattarelli 2005: 81ff.).

Mazzini's beliefs therefore also included many elements of Schulze-Delitzsch's socio-theoretical concept.

1843 Hotokusha, a farmers' and craftsmen's cooperative, was established in Japan. It was the country's first cooperative (see Centro italiano 2015).

1844 The first cooperative was established in Iceland; this was a consumer cooperative (see Centro italiano 2015).

This year also marked the end of three centuries of cooperative history, which we could call the incubation period for the modern cooperative system. What was in a sense rather naively begun by the North Italian actors of the Commedia dell'Arte in 1545 was completed quite deliberately by the Rochdale Pioneers in Central England in 1844. They - the 28 flannel weavers - founded the Rochdale Society of Equitable Pioneers, the most famous cooperative in the history of the international cooperative movement to date. Their shop in Toad Lane opened on 21 December 1844. The "equitable pioneers" went as far as defining the fundamental principles of cooperatives, later to be adopted - in modified form - by the International Co-operative Alliance. The four most important principles were and still are democratic control, open membership, fixed and limited interest on capital and distribution of the surplus as dividend on purchase. Luigi Luzzatti, Italy's most prominent cooperative figure of the 19th century, described the Rochdale Pioneers as the "saints of the cooperative movement" (see Cole 1944: 37ff.; Hasselmann 1971: 18ff.; Birchall 1997: 7; Totomianz and Wingler 1928: 751).

1845 The "Ermunterung[16]" was founded in Chemnitz; this was the first German consumer cooperative (see Hasselmann 1971: 41ff. and Katzenstein 1928b: 220).

A publication by historian Wilhelm Adolf Schmidt also appeared in the same year, in which Schmidt writes: "Pauperism, as we have seen, is the result of isolation [...] There is therefore no doubt as to what constitutes the next important step; that of breaking isolation without relinquishing liberty, without regression. And this is only possible through association, through free fraternisation in a truly moral sense, with the aims of mutual support or insurance. Only such an association can replace the material guarantees of unfree and dependent living conditions and guarantee their vital moral essence, without impairing the liberty and self-determination of the individual. It is the only means with which society itself can perpetually ward off destitution. This can indeed be everlasting provided its lifeblood does not run dry.

Just look at the many different insurance companies covering fire, the risks of trade and shipping, accidents during transportation of goods by land and sea, hail damage, livestock disease etc.! How do they differ from associations for the mutual guarantee of greater or lesser property? – Or look at the countless life insurances, pension institutions, widows' funds; at trade fund associations and those of other bourgeois classes, such as typesetters and printers, painters and school teachers; at the societies set up by travelling salesmen as protection from poverty and illness through no fault of their own, as they have existed in London for the past 45 years; at benefit societies for needy errand boys in Berlin amongst other places; at the association currently forming in Paris to support needy artists, such as historical and genre painters, sculptors and architects, engravers and illustrators; at foundations to support destitute doctors, such as the Hufeland'sche in Berlin; at the formation of a pension fund for old and weak intellectuals promised by Prussian synods, based on contributions from all intellectuals! What are they, if not

16 Encouragement

associations for the mutual support of members or their relatives?" (Schmidt 1845: 36 and 38).

These beliefs once again anticipate those of Schulze-Delitzsch, who also strived to achieve a rich network of associations to solve social issues.

1846 Bergsoe founded the first farmer's credit cooperative in Denmark (see Veiland-Haupt 1928: 164).

1847 William Howitt established the Cooperative League in London (see Totomianz 1928d: 148).

The cooperative credit institute "Darleihkasse" was founded in Mannheim (see Schulze-Delitzsch 1860: 18/19) and the "Creditkasse des Vereins für das Wohl der arbeitenden Klassen[17]" was established in Frankfurt/Oder (see Schulze-Delitzsch 1861: 18/19). Schulze-Delitzsch later stumbled across these cooperatives and incorporated them in his federation.

Jean Maurice Fibre founded the first Brazilian cooperative in Parana (see Centro italiano 2015).

1848 The first bakers' cooperatives were established in Belgium (see Centro italiano 2015).

Victor Aimé Huber published the essay "Selbsthülfe der arbeitenden Klassen durch Wirtschaftsvereine und innere Ansiedlung[18]" in his Berlin newspaper "Janus". Willy Krebs, an active member and advocate of Raiffeisen associations, later declared that Huber was "the first resolute German thinker of the cooperative system" (see Krebs 1928b: 463).

In Berlin, Ludwig Bisky, one of the leading revolutionaries and chairman of the Berlin "Arbeiterverbrüderung[19]", presented cooperative concepts at workers' conventions. Adolf Wuttig, an

---

17 Association for the Welfare of the Working Classes
18 Self-help of working classes through economic associations and internal ocupation
19 Workers`Brotherhood

ardent supporter of Raiffeisen, remarked of Bisky 60 years later "He is the true founder of our German cooperative system." (Wuttig 1907: 4).

Berlin's local "Arbeiterverbrüderung" committee established a "bread wholesale association" and "set up a central cooperative health insurance fund". Stephan Born, the main initiator of the "Arbeiterverbrüderung", saw a widespread cooperative-style organisation of society as the solution to social issues. "Born perceives his economic-cooperative organisations as a powerful means of transforming society, to eliminate class differences and establish a united production collective."(Kampffmeyer 1928: 124ff.).

The "Handwerkerdarlehnskasse zu Cöslin[20]" was also founded in 1848 in Cöslin. It was later incorporated into Schulze-Delitzsch's federation (see Schulze-Delitzsch 1861: 18/19).

Here ends our historical overview. This extremely brief summary of anthropological, prehistoric and historical findings clearly reveals that the cooperative idea has always been present throughout human evolution and in human societies, at least in latent form. Ivano Barberini's remark, at the beginning of this book, that cooperatives are in man's DNA, was therefore not as bold as it may initially have appeared. Cooperative interaction of people for the purpose of specific goals has always existed, long before it was developed into a general idea. Neanderthal horse hunters may have put cooperation into practice but the extent to which they were able to understand the underlying idea and possibly develop it, can be questioned. However, the cooperative idea was definitely rife by the time of Ancient Greece.

20 Cöslin Craftsmen´s Loan Society

Hermann Schulze-Delitzsch

Schulze-Delitzsch founded two purchasing cooperatives, one for carpenters and one for shoemakers, in his home town in 1849. They applied the principles of self-help and solidarity (see Stein 1928: 802). In the following year, Anton Bernhardi and Ernst Bürmann established "the first German credit cooperative with shared liability" in Eilenburg. In the same year, Schulze-Delitzsch set up a cooperative credit association in Delitzsch, initially based on donations. Later he developed it into a self-help cooperative (see Stein 1928: 802), adopting the principle of shared liability in line with the model in Eilenburg. (see Ruhmer 1928: 181). Contrary to all known facts, Schulze-Delitzsch's associations are described by the German cooperative system today as the first "modern" cooperatives.

How important was the role he then actually played in the never-ending history of cooperatives? He did nothing other than seize an idea that had been the subject of public discussion for decades in most parts of Europe, including Germany, and had already been put into practice in various different forms. Schulze-Delitzsch, a profoundly political man, saw cooperatives - his cooperatives - as an essential part of a widespread social movement which would solve the formidably pressing social issues of his time. These cooperatives were to do nothing less than promote the social and political emancipation of workers and craftsmen. This movement also included workers' educational associations, trade unions, aid funds (i.e. social insurance associations based on self-help) as well as economic cooperatives. Schulze-Delitzsch was actively involved in national education, fought for freedom of the press and universal suffrage and for more democracy. It was not without reason that he referred to cooperatives as "schools of democracy". He saw them - the cooperatives – as being part of an important liberal and democratic movement; producer cooperatives being the most important. He was co-founder of the liberal Progressive Party in Germany and initiated the founding of the first trade unions:

the trade associations. Cooperatives, just like the Liberal Party, were also part of the middle-class nationalist movement which aimed for German unification. Indeed Schulze-Delitzsch adopted a clearly nationalist tone at times (particularly towards Poland and France). Schulze-Delitzsch's eminence lies in the social and historical significance and extent of his commitment, as well as in the ardent and fearless manner in which he fought for his ideas in authoritarian Prussia and later in the German Reich (see Kaltenborn 2012a: passim; Kaltenborn 2012b: passim; Kaltenborn 2012c: passim; Kaltenborn 2014a: passim).

The principles that Schulze-Delitzsch demanded of cooperatives were: self-help; voluntary action, including resignation, i.e. open membership; self-management and an uppermost decision-making body consisting of all members; shared liability; no support from public and/or private means; equal distribution of profit and loss per capita; equal rights and obligations for all; a firm rejection of cumulative voting rights; formation of company shares. (see Schulze-Delitzsch 1853:4/5 and 40ff.; Schulze-Delitzsch 1863: 71ff., 111ff., 120, 124ff., 131; Schulze-Delitzsch 1870: 253; Schulze-Delitzsch 1876a: 162).

Measured in terms of his extensive socio-political and constitutional goals, Schulze-Delitzsch did not actually achieve very much. The social issues of his time may have been resolved, but only to a very limited extent by the self-help of the underprivileged classes. His democratic resolve is all but forgotten today. Even the modern-day cooperative system has little in common with Schulze-Delitzsch's intentions. It is not part of a widespread social movement and many statutory provisions actually blatantly contradict Schulze-Delitzsch's convictions: the option of cumulative voting rights, renunciation of universal distribution of profit per capita, the statutory provision allowing a delegates' meeting to replace a general meeting of all members, and enforced membership of auditing federations which has applied to German cooperatives since 1934 – Schulze-Delitzsch would have seen all of this as incompatible with the spirit of a free cooperative, as a school of democracy and a vehicle of emancipation.

The limitations imposed on the German cooperative system, in other words the large federations, by legislative restriction of the legal form to a registered cooperative society disavow the essence of Schulze-Delitzsch's beliefs. These blinkers shut out a colourful variety of examples of economic cooperation and civic organisations of all kinds, and in reality only harm the cooperative idea. (There is, however, one exception among the large federations of the Deutsche Genossenschafts- und Raiffeisenverband[21], namely the "Mittelstandsverbund – ZGV e. V.", that has around 230 affiliated associations, half of which do not have a cooperative legal form - see Kaltenborn 2014b: 296/297 and MGV 2015). If we wanted to take Schulze-Delitzsch seriously today, in a very different social and political context, it would first be necessary to ensure that "associations of separate small individual forces in the interest of common aims" are viewed as he – Schulze-Delitzsch – intended: as the implementation of the cooperative idea. This would undoubtedly boost recognition of the cooperative idea in society. One aspect of the Cooperative Societies Act can, however, be returned to its original purpose, in compliance with Schulze-Delitzsch's convictions, i.e. by revoking the mandatory affiliation of cooperatives to auditing federations which has been in force since October 1934. This enforced membership was part of National Socialist ideology (see Kaltenborn 2015: passim).

The fact that Schulze-Delitzsch is still referred to today by the official German cooperative system as the founder of the "modern" cooperative and held in high (if false) esteem, is obviously down to two reasons: he was the first to launch the initiative for a special cooperative law in Prussia (which was later extended to the whole of Germany) and fought for it passionately. This law of 1867 has since been subject to countless amendments; some of which have already been mentioned. It can, consequently, no longer be considered to be Schulze-

21 *The German Cooperative and Raiffeisen Confederation*

Delitzsch's law but may be ascribed to him. Secondly, Schulze-Delitzsch founded a federation of German cooperatives as early as 1859 which, asides from a short interruption after 1945, has never ceased to exist, not even during the period of National Socialist dictatorship. Schulze-Delitzsch therefore left two lasting marks which engendered a long-standing reputation - however objectively justified this may be.

Friedrich Wilhelm Raiffeisen

Raiffeisen established a benefit society with wealthy residents in Weyerbusch (Westerwald) in 1846. It purchased flour and baked bread which was then sold to the poor at half the price; the society later also sold cheap seed (see Raiffeisen 1887: 4 and Krebs 1928a: 714ff.). This was, however, still quite a step from the idea and practice of the cooperative.

Two years later, he set up another aid society with the help of around 60 of the "wealthiest residents of the district" in Flammersfeld (also Westerwald), this time to procure cattle for poor farmers. Members had "equal" liability (see Raiffeisen 1872: 10/11; see also Krebs 1928a: 714ff.). There is still no question of self-help, nor does it resemble the cooperative concept Raiffeisen later advocated.

Four years later, four "winegrowers' cooperatives (were established) along the Moselle river on a pure cooperative basis" as a result of private and governmental initiatives. These winegrowers' associations already used the name "cooperative". They practised open membership and collective business operations. This involved the purchase of shared wine cellars and the handling and supervision of the wine stored there. Members had joint liability. There was no profit-sharing. All profit was assigned to the reserve fund. The area of operation of each association was identical to that of a parish. "These associations were plainly purchasing and trade organisations. [...]

The similarity between Raiffeisen's later work and that undertaken earlier by the winegrowers is quite blatant." (Blesius 1929: 19ff.).

Raiffeisen was responsible for founding the "Heddesdorfer Wohltätigkeitsverein[22]" in 1854. Once again it was supported by wealthy residents. The Heddesdorf Society provided for the upbringing of abandoned children, found work for the unemployed, particularly ex-convicts, and finally founded a credit bank (see Raiffeisen 1872: 11). Willy Krebs, a leading member of the Raiffeisen organisation itself, later declared that the three associations in Weyerbusch, Flammersfeld and Heddesdorf were merely "charitable institutions and not ones of 'self-help'. The step to an actual cooperative was only taken when those in need became the actual members and assumed joint liability". (Krebs 1928c: 852/853).

Gradually, Raiffeisen recognised "that those associations built upon the principle of charity were not viable. However, he did not abandon his efforts to combat rural misery and looked for a sustainable form of organisation instead."   In 1862, he had "finally found a suitable model for the establishment of rural cooperatives. He subsequently founded credit unions for the parish of Anhausen and for that of Rengsdorf and Bonefeld, for Engers Town Hall and the Upper County of Wied." (Blesius 1929: 12/13; see also Zeidler 1893: 121/122). Raiffeisen noted at that time "I was reluctant to abandon the idea that associations should be founded on the basis of Christian duty and brotherly love, rather than on self-interest." However, he had to admit that Schulze-Delitzsch was right and "that such associations can only be viable and lasting if they are founded on unconditional self-help, i.e. members may only be those who personally need help. [...] In recognition of this fact, Raiffeisen then reorganised the Heddesdorf Society on the model of Schulze's credit and loan societies [...]." (see Blesius 1929: 14ff.).

22 Heddesdorf Charitable Society

The Heddesdorf Society was re-established in 1864. It was now an institution of self-help, with admission fees, business shares, distribution of profit and (as before) an indivisible reserve fund. It now only dealt in loan transactions. (see Raiffeisen 1872: 12ff.; Blesius 1929: 15).

The years 1862/64 can be seen as marking the beginning of the real Raiffeisen cooperatives.

Raiffeisen did not, however, introduce any new ideas to the history of cooperatives. Driven by his profoundly Christian desire to help the poorest rural folk of his home town, he began at the first opportunity to encourage the wealthy to fulfil their Christian duty and make financial donations to institutions, namely aid societies, for different measures, such as the purchase of cattle, the education of abandoned children and the use of new agricultural machines and methods. It took him years to finally find the right approach. His method was one of trial and error.

Raiffeisen's eminence lies in the fervour of his combat to overcome economic and moral poverty in his home town, to the point of self-disregard (see Koch 1986: 16ff.). He considered his actions to be nothing more than the strict application of his Christian faith (see Raiffeisen 1922: 11). The intensity of his beliefs, not to say religious fundamentalism, pushed to him to aim for a theocracy (see Schäfer 2010: 6 and 14ff.). He wrote in 1887 "It is primarily a matter, not of ephemeral earthly happiness, but of aspiring to eternal heavenly blessings. Christ himself has shown us the way through his teachings and example." (Raiffeisen 1887: 2). Raiffeisen showed less evidence of the kind of extensive theoretical reflections developed by Schulze-Delitzsch. One uglier side of Raiffeisen did, however, develop in this context - his anti-Semitism (see Kaltenborn 2014b: 69ff.). Aside from this, Raiffeisen's beliefs resemble those of Johann Friedrich Oberlin in many ways.

Raiffeisen's final cooperative model applied the following principles: self-help; open membership; joint liability; no fees, no dividends, no business shares; sponsorship of associations by the wealthy; limitation of membership and area of action to a (church) parish; better education and training; more efficient forms of soil cultivation; application of Christian principles in cooperatives (see Raiffeisen 1872: preface and Zeidler 1893: 121ff.).

To what does Raiffeisen then owe his lasting fame, if he contributed nothing or very little to the cooperative idea? Mention should first be made of how his actions concentrated on agriculture and his region. Then there are his close ties with the church, primarily the Catholic Church, although Raiffeisen was in fact protestant. The priest was generally also the "accountant" of the local Raiffeisen bank. Georg Eucken-Addenhausen, the Oldenburg emissary in Berlin, observed "that no profession had proved to be a truer, more successful manager of the Raiffeisen credit societies than the clergy" (quoted in Wuttig 1907: 20). He also added that the Raiffeisen cooperatives soon adopted a dual approach as "in addition to granting loans, the joint procurement of agricultural raw materials, such as fertiliser, animal feed, seeds etc. became the most important line of business." (Zeidler 1893: 295).

Finally, the Raiffeisen movement also received official support, initially from the Prussian authorities in the Rhineland, due to its early success in combatting rural poverty (see Schneider 2005: 313/314). The continuing growth of Raiffeisen associations (which increased both in number and importance) was "particularly encouraged and supported by the goodwill of government and administrative authorities, which either directly endorsed the movement or promoted its development through exemption or relief from taxes, fees etc." (Zeidler 1893: 295). In 1880, the Prussian Minister for Agriculture, Robert Lucius, even instructed Raiffeisen to tour the poorest districts of Silesia and compile a report (see Zeidler 1893: 296). Raiffeisen and his cooperatives were not opposed to political authority, unlike the Schulze-Delitzsch movement. The final reason for Raiffeisen's lasting reputation is probably the speed with which his system was adopted abroad. Raiffeisen appeared almost surprised when he observed at the end of the 1880s that "interest in the associations is also growing in other European countries, with few exceptions". This was evident from "articles in public prints". Such interest was shown in Russia, the Netherlands, Belgium, Spain, France, Denmark, Switzerland, Italy, Austria-Hungary. (see Raiffeisen 1887: XIII).

Schulze-Delitzsch and Raiffeisen seen by early cooperative historians

Interestingly, earlier authors who studied the origins and developments of cooperatives were still aware of the true beginnings of the more recent cooperative system.

Hans Crüger, for example, observed in 1898 "Schulze-Delitzsch did not invent cooperatives". His merit lay in the fact that he "adapted it [...] to modern conditions and requirements". (Crüger 1898: 10). Crüger had been the "Legal Counsellor" (in other words Chairman) of the "Allgemeiner Verband der deutschen Erwerbs- und Wirtschaftsgenossenschaften[23]" founded by Schulze-Delitzsch, since 1896. He was also a member of same liberal Progressive Party as Schulze-Delitzsch and held the same seat at the Reichstag in his day (for a modified constituency).

Friedrich Müller wrote a comprehensive history of the agricultural cooperative system in 1901, a movement for which he showed great affinity. In it, he wrote that Raiffeisen's societies were "by no means the only, and undoubtedly not the first institutions of their kind at that time [...], but were just examples of a form of association which had already frequently existed in many areas of Germany before 1850". (Müller 1901: 27).

---

23 General Federation of German Commercial and Trading Cooperatives

Adolf Wuttig was even more explicit in his comments on Schulze-Delitzsch's foundations when he wrote that the "institutions in Delitzsch" were just copies (see Wuttig 1907: 4). Richard Finck expressed a similar opinion, although not quite so drastically, in a benevolent overview of Schulze-Delitzsch's cooperative system: "The cooperative idea was already in the air in the 1840s." (Finck 1909: 12).

Willy Wygodzinski, another advocate of cooperative ideas and principles, said in a general presentation of the cooperative system: "Neither Schulze nor Raiffeisen, however great their merits may be, were the founders of the cooperative system, but it was the result of ancient instincts, lying dormant in the bosom of mankind, and economic expediency." (Wygodzinski 1911: 6).

A situation is sometimes best understood by making a comparison. Lego bricks, for example, have existed for decades - as the accomplishment of an idea. They come in many colours and sizes. When our granddaughter first got hold of them, she selected the colours and sizes she liked best, the number of bricks she wanted, and built whatever she fancied. When applied to the history of cooperatives, it means that Schulze-Delitzsch and Raiffeisen checked the principles, methods and structures they had found in many earlier cooperative concepts and achievements, and then selected and compiled those that would enable them to achieve the cooperative model best suited to their main social and socio-political aims. This is an undeniable fact.

Schulze-Delitzsch himself was of no other opinion. There can be no doubt, he said, "that we, in Germany, still fall far short of the progress made by the associative system in England and France." (Schulze-Delitzsch 1853: 90). He played down his own role quite modestly when he observed that some craftsmen had "drawn closer to the guiding principle of the other workers, i.e. self-help [...]. This had prepared the ground for local special-purpose cooperatives, the economic and trade associations, and it took just a prod to steer the prevailing trend of the working classes in this direction." (Schulze-Delitzsch 1858: 82/83).

The broad interpretation of the term 'cooperative' before 1933

Both the earlier name "association" and the later term "cooperative", which was more commonly used after 1860, had a wide definition in the eyes of all of the above, including Schulze-Delitzsch. Cooperative meant "cooperative action" regardless of the form. It is therefore logical that relevant literature of that time also referred, for example, to private limited companies (GmbH) as cooperatives. "The legal form used to establish a workers' cooperative has no particular impact on its inner spirit", if the statutes are sufficiently based on cooperative principles. (see Schembor 1921: 140ff.; see also Kaltenborn 2014b: 146ff. and 158ff.). Schulze-Delitzsch was of the same opinion. He published a list of all cooperatives known to him in 1879, which included partnerships limited by shares (KGaA), joint-stock companies (AG) and general partnerships (OHG) (see Schulze-Delitzsch 1879: 11/12).

The key question in Germany before 1933 was to what extent true cooperation actually existed, i.e. identical rights, identical burdens and identical advantages. It was a well-known fact that the idea of cooperative action and cooperative economic activity had always existed throughout the history of mankind, independently of the conditions and circumstances of the economy. The idea itself is nothing special but the respective form it takes is. Every age and society adopts its own model.

The socio-political dimension of cooperatives

What characterises the newer (if you like: more modern) cooperatives, e.g. since the end of the 18th century, compared to their predecessors, is the expectation of being able to create a better society through a widespread cooperative system. "Better" can of course mean different things: more just, more humane, more democratic or even more efficient.

This hope that cooperatives could contribute to a better world was certainly not alive in Ancient Greece, or amongst the actors of the Commedia dell'Arte. However, it was definitely alive in John Bellers at the end of the 17th century, and later in Johann Friedrich Oberlin, Heinrich Pestalozzi, Charles Fourier, Heinrich Zschokke, Robert Owen and William King, in Philippe Buchez and Louis Blanc, in Giuseppe Mazzini and finally in Viktor Aimé Huber, Friedrich Wilhelm Raiffeisen and Hermann Schulze-Delitzsch in Germany. It is still expressed by the International Co-operative Alliance today, but is also present in many different groups and organisations throughout the globe. The exact expectations of what and how cooperatives could contribute to furthering society do however vary. There is no generally accepted concept for this, making it very difficult to agree on what cooperatives are meant to achieve. In fact, not all advocates of cooperatives actually want to improve society, preferring to just better their own personal situation within it.

The fundamental shortcomings of the nomination

Let us now take a look at some of the key statements in the nomination by the German Commission for UNESCO and the scope of these claims. However, it is important to note that the German Commission for UNESCO did not think up the reasons stated in the nomination on its own. It based them on the claim submitted by two German cooperative institutions - the "Deutsche Hermann-

Schulze-Delitzsch-Gesellschaft[24]" and the "Deutsche Friedrich-Wilhelm-Raiffeisen-Gesellschaft[25]". Both these societies supplied the arguments and German wording which the Commission then adapted into English and submitted to UNESCO in Paris.

These two cooperative societies are, therefore, responsible for the claim that the idea and practice of cooperatives spread from Delitzsch, Weyerbusch and Flammersfeld to other parts of Germany and beyond, and that it is practiced nearly worldwide today. However, it would appear that this claim to German ownership of the cooperative idea was not entirely free from doubt as the text later declares that "the idea for the first cooperative organizations goes back to the Welshman Robert Owen". Such contradictions reveal an extremely disinterested treatment of historical facts. So is the cooperative idea Welsh or German for the two societies? Or does it not matter? Or should the reader just toss a coin? Delitzsch must of course be mentioned in the history of cooperatives, just as Weyerbusch and Flammersfeld should appear in every biography of Raiffeisen. The cooperative idea, however, is only an incomer in all three places.

The fact that the German word "Genossenschaftsidee" (cooperative idea) is translated into English as "the idea and practice of organizing shared interests in cooperatives" has already been mentioned. Cooperative practice in Germany – and not just there – has constantly evolved over the years and will continue to do so. It is strange to imagine that the justification for intangible cultural heritage of humanity can be subject to continuing changes, depending, for example, on whether or not the German legislator considers it necessary and expedient to adapt the Cooperative Societies Act to an existing context.

The nomination continues by stating that over 20 million members and 863,000 employees of cooperatives in Germany "are actively involved with the daily practice and transmission of the idea and practice". This is pure ideology. In practice, however,

24 German Hermann Schulze Delitzsch Society
25 Germann Friedrich Wilhelm Raiffeisen Society

things look very different. Can you imagine what would happen, for example, if the one hundred thousand members of the Berlin Volksbank were actively involved in the daily practice and transmission of the cooperative idea? You read me correctly: one hundred thousand people actively involved in that task! They would never get round to any proper banking business.

It is also completely unrealistic to claim that members "work together on a voluntary basis for the benefit of all". Do the members of the Berlin (or Wiesbaden or Leipzig or any other) Volksbank work together for the benefit of all? How does this happen in practical terms? This type of phrase is easy to write but not so easy to believe.

For almost a century now, it has been legally possible in Germany for cooperatives of a certain size to adopt a delegates' meeting in place of a general meeting of all cooperative members. This affects the large majority of all cooperative members. Take the Volksbanks as an example: almost 18 million of the total 22 million cooperative members (2013) alone (i.e. over 80 %) are members of cooperative banks (see Stappel 2014: 8). With the exception of very small, rural Raiffeisen banks, the Volksbanks have long since abandoned general meetings in favour of a delegates' meeting. In spite of this, the two societies prefer to ignore the facts by claiming that every member normally has a vote at the general meeting.

The nomination's statement that Schulze-Delitzsch and Raiffeisen founded non-profit cooperative banks is also false. The credit cooperatives had to be profitable from the start. How else could they have promoted the economic activities of their members, which was after all their task, in fact their legally established task? Schulze-Delitzsch even set up model calculations: a business volume of 80,000 thalers required a capital of 20,000 thalers. A net profit of 1,200 thalers should and could therefore be recorded. If the entire capital was raised by members, a six per cent interest rate was given (see Schulze-Delitzsch 1876b: 98). This has nothing to do with a non-profit organisation.

Raiffeisen did not exactly encourage dividend payments to members but accepted them if this was what the members wanted (see Raiffeisen 1872: 1ff.).

It is beyond comprehension and quite grotesque that the "Deutsche Hermann-Schulze-Delitzsch-Gesellschaft" and "Deutsche Friedrich-Wilhelm-Raiffeisen-Gesellschaft" made a false statement to the German Commission for UNESCO regarding the simplest and plainest fact relating to the German cooperative system: the number of German cooperatives. The UNESCO nomination indicates 5,800 (see Deutsche UNESCO 2015a, as well as for all quotes or references relating to the nomination). There were in fact almost 40 % more in 2014, i.e. 8,007 cooperatives (see Stappel 2014: 8). This figure – like many others – can be found in the well-organised and extremely comprehensible annual publication "Die deutschen Genossenschaften[26]". It is published by the Deutscher Genossenschafts-Verlag[27], and can quite rightly be considered an official cooperative publication, and is also available online.

The entire nomination and its justifications give the impression that none of the participants supported it with any real interest, knowledge, understanding or even passion. It was in fact mistaken in its approach when declaring the cooperative idea to be intangible cultural heritage of humanity. What it should have done was consider the deliberate, cooperative, equitable interaction of men in the interests of a common goal, or rather the idea behind it, without insisting on a specific form. That would really have been intangible cultural heritage of humanity. Delitzsch, Weyerbusch and Flammersfeld would then have no business in the justification. The appropriate anthropological, prehistoric and historical findings would have to be presented – in a much more stringent manner than here - and the truly astounding capacity for "association of separate small individual forces in the interest of common aims" that has always existed throughout the evolution and history of mankind, from the

26 The German Cooperatives
27 German Cooperatives Publishing House

Neanderthal hunters to the informal dairy cooperative founded in UvurOrgioch, Mongolia in 2006 (see ICA-AP 2015), should be at the heart of the nomination and its justifications.

Summary

Hermann Schulze-Delitzsch labelled the cooperative idea as the "association of separate small individual forces in the interest of common aims".

Cooperative theorists and founders of cooperatives have always considered cooperative interaction as belonging to human nature: "The history of mankind is also the history of association".

Scientific anthropology confirms such statements.

Man's ability to cooperate, to achieve "common goals" was already visible in early man, whether in Homo habilis or Homo neanderthalensis or in the very first Homo sapiens.

Cooperative forms with quite modern characteristics (pursuit of common goals, self-management, voluntary action, democratic decision-making processes) could be found in Ancient Greece and in Ancient Rome.

Schulze-Delitzsch believed that the Germanic peoples possessed an extensive cooperative system whose "characteristic features" were similar to those of the cooperative movement he initiated in Germany.

Rural cooperatives played an important role in large parts of medieval Europe. Without them, the three-field system, advanced for its time, would have been inconceivable.

In the 19th century, German jurists undertook intensive research into the traditional idea and practice of cooperatives, parallel to Schulze-Delitzsch and Raiffeisen (and independently of them).

In the mid-16th century, a new era of modern cooperatives began in Northern Italy with a Commedia dell'Arte theatre troupe.

At the end of the 17th century, John Bellers developed the cooperative idea with social reform goals.

The cooperative idea was represented in literature from the end of the 18th century onwards.

By the middle of the 19th century, cooperative establishments were known to exist in Poland, the USA, France, Scotland, Greece, England, Austria, Italy, Luxembourg, Switzerland, Ireland, Russia, Spain, Iceland, Germany, Japan, the Czech provinces of Austria-Hungary, Brazil, Denmark and Belgium.

In 1821, the first cooperative newspaper was published in England and the first English Cooperative Congress was held in Manchester in 1831. 266 cooperatives existed in England at that time.

By the mid-19th century, John Bellers, Johann Friedrich Oberlin, Carl Gottlieb Suarez, Heinrich Pestalozzi, Charles Fourier, Heinrich Zschokke, Robert Owen, William King, Philippe Buchez, Louis Blanc, Giuseppe Mazzini and Viktor Aimé Huber had addressed the cooperative idea in theory, practice or in literature, and were then followed by Friedrich Wilhelm Raiffeisen and Hermann Schulze-Delitzsch.

The year 1844 marked the peak of the modern cooperative movement with the founding of the "Rochdale Society of Equitable Pioneers" in Central England. The cooperative principles defined in Rochdale still apply in the international cooperative movement today. No new notions have been added with regard to the overall character of the cooperative idea since Rochdale. The International Co-operative Alliance endorsed these principles once again, on the occasion of their centenary in Manchester in 1995.

Schulze-Delitzsch founded his first cooperatives in his home town in 1849/1850.

Raiffeisen established his cooperative model in 1862/64, having first experimented with mere aid societies since 1846 in his efforts to alleviate rural poverty.

None of the main principles which applied to cooperatives founded by Raiffeisen und Schulze-Delitzsch were developed by the founders. Raiffeisen and Schulze-Delitzsch merely gave specific shape to the importance of these principles.

Neither of the two, not Schulze-Delitzsch nor Raiffeisen, developed the cooperative idea, as German cooperative literature duly observed at the end of the 19th century and turn of the 20th century.

Both Raiffeisen and Schulze-Delitzsch wanted to achieve more than just economic benefits for members of cooperatives. Raiffeisen wanted his movement to strengthen Christian spirit amongst the rural population. Schulze-Delitzsch wanted to solve the social issues of his time through a federation of all types of cooperatives including trade unions, educational associations, national movements, liberal institutions, and to achieve the unity of the German nation through democratic organisations.

Cooperatives, i.e. cooperative human interaction for the purpose of common goals (objectives) of both economic and social nature, have existed throughout the history and evolution of mankind and will continue to do so in the future.

Legal forms only a play an official role. They do not constitute the implementation of the cooperative idea.

Bibliography

Aretin, Christoph Freiherr von (1823): Ausführliche Darstellung der baierischen Kredit-Vereins-Anstalt und ihrer Bedingnisse sowohl für die Gutsbesitzer als auch für die Kapitalisten. Munich.

Aristoteles (1971): Politik. Introduction, translation and comments by Olof Gigon. 2nd revised edition, extended by one comment. Zurich and Stuttgart.

Barberini, Ivano (2009): Come vola il calabrone. Cooperazione, etica e sviluppo. Milano.

Becker, Rudolf Zacharias (1786): Die Kunst, Leute zu schröpfen, die noch nicht geboren sind. Eine Lobrede auf die Todten-Cassen und Trauerpfennigs-, Denk- und Sterbethaler-Genossenschaften. In einem patriotischen Clubb an der Weser gehalten am 1. April 1786. Gotha.

Bernstein, Eduard (1922): Sozialismus und Demokratie in der großen englischen Revolution. 4th illustraded ed. Berlin.

Beseler, Georg (1885): System des gemeinen deutschen Privatrechts. Two volumes, 4th enhanced and improved ed. Berlin.

Bick, Almut (2012): Die Steinzeit. Extended reprint. Stuttgart.

Birchall, Johnston (1997): The international co-operative Movement. Manchester and New York.

Bischof-Köhler, Doris (2009): Empathie. In: Eike Bohlken and Christian Thies (eds.): Handbuch Anthropologie. Der Mensch zwischen Natur, Kultur und Technik. Stuttgart and Weimar.

Blanc, Louis (1899): Organisation der Arbeit. Translation based on the 9th revised version of the original, enhanced by one chapter. Berlin.

Blesius, Nikolaus (1929): Zur Entstehungsgeschichte des neuzeitlichen ländlichen Genossenschaftswesens. Vortrag gehalten im Seminar für Genossenschaftswesen und Handelskunde der landwirtschaftl. Hochschule zu Berlin. Berlin.

Centro italiano (2015): Centro italiano di documentazione sulla cooperazione e l'economia sociale: http://www.cooperazione.net/pagina.asp?pid=363. Consulted online on 04.05.2015.

Chalmel, Loic (2012). Oberlin: Ein Pfarrer der Aufklärung. Potsdam and Waldersbach.

Cocco, Ester (1915): Una Compagnia comica nella prima metà del secolo XVI. In: Giornale Storico della Letteratura Italiana, Magazine no. 65.

Cole, George Douglas Howard (1944): A Century of Co-operation. Manchester.

Crüger, Hans (1898): Der heutige Stand des deutschen Genossenschaftswesens. Berlin.

Daudé-Bancel, Achille (1928): Frankreich. Die französischen Konsumgenossenschaften. In: Vahan Totomianz (ed.): Internationales Handwörterbuch des Genossenschaftswesens. Berlin.

Delius, Walter (1909): Zur Rechtsgeschichte und Dogmatik der Hauberge und Haubergsgenossenschaften des Siegerlandes. Abhandlung zur Erlangung der juristischen Doktorwürde der Hohen juristischen Fakultät der Rheinischen Friedrich-Wilhelms-Universität zu Bonn. Breslau.

Dettelbacher, Werner (1988): Bauern und Agrarwirtschaft. In: Heinrich Pleticha (ed.): Deutsche Geschichte in 12 Bänden. Vol. 2 Von den Saliern zu den Staufern 1024 – 1152. Gütersloh.

Deutsche UNESCO (2015a): www.unesco.de/fileadmin/medien/Dokumente/Kultur/IKE/ICH -02-2016EN_Germany.pdf. Consulted online on 05.05.2015.

Deutsche UNESCO (2015b): www.unesco.de/kultur/2015/nominierung-genossenschaften.html. Consulted online on 16.06.2015.

Faucherre, Henry (1928): Zschokke. In: Vahan Totomianz (ed.): Internationales Handwörterbuch des Genossenschaftswesens. Berlin.

Finck, Richard (1909): Das Schulze-Delitzsch'sche Genossenschaftswesen und die modernen genossenschaftlichen Entwickelungstendenzen. Jena.

Fiser, Albert (1928): Tschechoslowakei. Genossenschaften der Arbeiterschaft. In: Vahan Totomianz (eds.): Internationales Handwörterbuch des Genossenschaftswesens. Berlin.

Gaumont, Jean (1928): Paris. In: Vahan Totomianz (ed.): Internationales Handwörterbuch des Genossenschaftswesens. Berlin.

Gemeinschaftswaldgesetz (2015): www.wald-wuergendorf.de/ pdf/Gemeinschaftswaldgesetz.pdf. Consulted online on 15.09.2015|

Gide, Charles (1928): Buchez. In: Vahan Totomianz (ed.): Internationales Handwörterbuch des Genossenschaftswesens. Berlin.

Gierke, Otto Friedrich von (1881): Das deutsche Genossenschaftsrecht. Vol. 3: Die Staats- und Korporationslehre des Altertums und des Mittelalters und ihre Aufnahme in Deutschland. Berlin.

Großheim, Michael und Christian Thies (2009): Phänomenologie. In: Eike Bohlken and Christian Thies (eds.): Handbuch Anthropologie. Der Mensch zwischen Natur, Kultur und Technik. Stuttgart and Weimar.

Harari, Yuval Noah (2015): A brief history of Mankind. Munich.

Hasselmann, Erwin (1971): Geschichte der deutschen Konsumgenossenschaften. Frankfurt/Main.

ICA (2013): http://ica.coop/en/what-co-op/history-co-operative-movement. Consulted online on 13.10.2013.

ICA-AP (2015): http://www.ica-ap.coop/icaevents/visit-co-operatives-mongolia. Consulted online on 04.11.2015.

Jörke, Dirk (2009): Zoon politikon. In: Eike Bohlken and Christian Thies (eds.): Handbuch Anthropologie. Der Mensch zwischen Natur, Kultur und Technik. Stuttgart and Weimar.

Kaltenborn, Wilhelm (2012a): Schulze-Delitzsch und die soziale Frage. In: Wilhelm Kaltenborn: Vision und Wirklichkeit. Beiträge zur Idee und Geschichte von Genossenschaften. Berlin.

Kaltenborn, Wilhelm (2012b): Schulze-Delitzsch und die Arbeiterbewegung. In: Wilhelm Kaltenborn: Vision und Wirklichkeit. Beiträge zur Idee und Geschichte von Genossenschaften. Berlin.

Kaltenborn, Wilhelm (2012c): Ein großes deutsches Leben. In: Wilhelm Kaltenborn: Vision und Wirklichkeit. Beiträge zur Idee und Geschichte von Genossenschaften. Berlin.

Kaltenborn, Wilhelm (2014a): Nationalität und Nationalstaat bei Hermann Schulze-Delitzsch. In: Juhani Laurinkari et al (eds.): Genossenschaftswissenschaft zwischen Theorie und Geschichte. Festschrift für Prof. Dr. Johann Brazda zum 60. Geburtstag. Bremen.

Kaltenborn, Wilhelm (2014b): Schein und Wirklichkeit. Genossenschaften und Genossenschaftsverbände. Eine kritische Auseinandersetzung. Berlin.

Kaltenborn, Wilhelm (2015): Verdrängte Vergangenheit. Die historischen Wurzeln des Anschlusszwanges der Genossenschaften an Prüfungsverbände. Norderstedt.

Kampffmeyer, Paul (1928): Born. In: Vahan Totomianz (ed.): Internationales Handwörterbuch des Genossenschaftswesens. Berlin.

Katzenstein, Simon (1928a): Arbeiterbewegung und Genossenschaftsbewegung. In: Vahan Totomianz (ed.): Internationales Handwörterbuch des Genossenschaftswesens. Berlin.

Katzenstein, Simon (1928b): Ermunterung. In: Vahan Totomianz (ed.): Internationales Handwörterbuch des Genossenschaftswesens. Berlin.

Kern, Bernd-Rüdiger (1998): Genossenschaft. § 2 Rechtliches. In: Johannes Hoops: Reallexikon der Germanischen Altertumskunde. 2nd completely revised and extended edition. Berlin and New York.

Koch, Walter (1986): Was ihr getan habt einem dieser meiner geringsten Brüder, das habt ihr mir getan. In: Friedrich Wilhelm Raiffeisen: Briefe 1875 – 1883. Revised by Walöter Koch. Vienna.

Kornemann, Ernst (1901): Collegium. In: Georg Wissowa (ed.): Paulys Realencyclopädie der classischen Altertumswissenschaft. New revision, Vol. 4. Stuttgart.

Krebs, Willy: Raiffeisen (1928a). In: Vahan Totomianz (ed.): Internationales Handwörterbuch des Genossenschaftswesens. Berlin.

Krebs, Willy (1928b): Huber. In: Vahan Totomianz (ed.): Internationales Handwörterbuch des Genossenschaftswesens. Berlin.

Krebs, Willy (1928c): Spar- und Darlehnskassen-Vereine. In: Vahan Totomianz (ed.): Internationales Handwörterbuch des Genossenschaftswesens. Berlin.

Kulemann, Wilhelm (1922): Die Genossenschaftsbewegung. Vol. 1 Geschichtlicher Teil. Berlin.

Lang-Hinrichsen, Dietrich (1955): Beseler, Georg Karl Christoph. In: Neue Deutsche Biographie 2. Consulted online: http://www.deutsche-biographie.de/ppn118510193.html. 27.07.2015.

Lüning, Jens (2002): Grundlagen sesshaften Lebens. In: von Freden, Uta u. Siegmar Schnurbein: Spuren der Jahrtausende. Archäologie und Geschichte in Deutschland. Stuttgart.

Manfredi, F. (1928): Mazzini. In: Vahan Totomianz (ed.): Internationales Handwörterbuch des Genossenschaftswesens. Berlin.

Mattarelli, Sauro (2005): Dialogo sui doveri. Il pensiero di Giuseppe Mazzini. Venezia.

Mehnert, Henning (2003): Commedia dell'arte. Struktur – Geschichte – Rezeption. Stuttgart.

MGV (2015): www.mittelstandsverbund.de/Verband/Ziele-und-Aufgaben/DER-MITTELSTANDSVERBUND-Stark-fuer-den-kooperierenden-mittelstand-K113.htm. Consulted online on 20.11.2015.

Müller, Friedrich (1901): Die geschichtliche Entwicklung des landwirtschaftlichen Genossenschaftswesens in Deutschland von 1848/49 bis zur Gegenwart. Leipzig.

Müller, Hans (1928a): Altertum, Genossenschaftswesen im Altertum. In: Vahan Totomianz (ed.): Internationales Handwörterbuch des Genossenschaftswesens. Berlin.

Müller, Hans (1928b): Bellers. In: Vahan Totomianz (ed.): Internationales Handwörterbuch des Genossenschaftswesens. Berlin.

Müller-Beck, Hansjürgen (2004): Die Steinzeit. Der Weg der Menschen in die Geschichte. 3rd improved ed. Munich.

Ostner (2009), Julia: Primatologie. In: Eike Bohlken and Christian Thies (eds.): Handbuch Anthropologie. Der Mensch zwischen Natur, Kultur und Technik. Stuttgart and Weimar.

Pederzani-Weber, Julius (1888): Giuseppe Mazzini und seine Ideen zur Linderung des sozialen Elends. Berlin.

Pestalozzi, Johann Heinrich (1933): Lienhard and Gertrud. Bielefeld and Leipzig.

Platon (1921): Briefe. Translated and commented by Otto Apelt. 2nd revised ed. Leipzig.

Poland, Franz (1909): Geschichte des griechischen Vereinswesens. Gekrönte Preisschrift. Leipzig.

Raiffeisen, Friedrich Wilhelm (1872): Die Darlehnskassen-Vereine, in Verbindung mit Consum-, Verkaufs-, Gant- etc. Genossenschaften, als Mittel zur Abhilfe der Noth der ländlichen Bevölkerung, sowie auch der städtischen Arbeiter. 2nd ed. Neuwied.

Raiffeisen, Friedrich Wilhelm (1887): Die Darlehnskassen-Vereine in Verbindung mit Consum-, Verkaufs-, Winzer-, Molkerei-, Viehversicherungs- etc. Genossenschaften sowie den dazu gehörigen Instruktionen als Mittel zur Abhülfe der Noth der ländlichen Bevölkerung. Praktische Anleitung zur Gründung und Leitung solcher Genossenschaften. Erster Theil: Die Darlehnskassen-Vereine und sonstige ländliche Genossenschaften. 5th partly revised and improved ed. Neuwied.

Raiffeisen, Friedrich Wilhelm (1922): Raiffeisen-Worte. Auszüge aus den Schriften, Reden und Briefen F. W. Raiffeisens. 2nd ed. Neuwied.

Röhrken, Walter (1928): Oberlin. In: Vahan Totomianz (ed.): Internationales Handwörterbuch des Genossenschaftswesens. Berlin.

Rösener, Werner (1985): Bauern im Mittelalter. Munich.

Ruhmer, Otto (1928): Delitzsch, Darlehnskassenverein. In: Vahan Totomianz (ed.): Internationales Handwörterbuch des Genossenschaftswesens. Berlin.

Schäfer, Albert (2010): Friedrich Wilhelm Raiffeisen der Volkserzieher. Hachenburg.

Schembor, Otto (1921): Die genossenschaftliche Gemeinwirtschaft: Entstehung, Arten, Aufgaben und Arbeitsweise, Stand und Ausbaumöglichkeiten. Dresden.

Schmidt, Wilhelm Adolf (1845): Die Zukunft der arbeitenden Klassen und die Vereine für ihr Wohl. Eine Mahnung an die Zeitgenossen. Berlin.

Schneider, Karlheinz (2005): Judentum und Modernisierung. Ein deutsch-amerikanischer Vergleich 1870 – 1920. Frankfurt am Main.

Schnyder, Albert (2015): Zelgensysteme [in: Historisches Lexikon der Schweiz]. Consulted online under http://www.hls-dhs-dss.ch/textes/d/D13702.php, 03.10.2015.

Schreiber (1928): Mühlen- und Müllergenossenschaften. In:
Vahan Totomianz (ed.): Internationales Handwörterbuch des
Genossenschaftswesens. Berlin.

Schultze, Richard Sigmund (1867): Die Selbsthülfe, ihre
Entwicklung und Erfolge in den Genossenschaften. Greifswald.

Schulze-Delitzsch, Hermann (1853): Associationsbuch für
deutsche Handwerker. Leipzig.

Schulze-Delitzsch, Hermann (1858): Die arbeitenden Klassen und
das Associationswesen in Deutschland als Programm zu einem
deutschen Congress. Leipzig.

Schulze-Delitzsch, Hermann (1860): Jahresbericht für 1859 über
die auf dem Princip der Selbsthülfe der Betheiligten
beruhenden deutschen Genossenschaften der Handwerker und
Arbeiter. Leipzig.

Schulze-Delitzsch, Hermann (1861): Jahresbericht für 1860 über
die auf Selbsthülfe der Betheiligten gegründeten deutschen
Erwerbs- und Wirthschaftgenossenschaften des kleinen
Gewerbstandes. Leipzig.

Schulze-Delitzsch, Hermann (1863): Capitel zu einem deutschen
Arbeiterkatechismus. Sechs Vorträge vor dem Berliner
Arbeiterverein. Leipzig.

Schulze-Delitzsch, Hermann (1865): Die nationale Bedeutung der
deutschen Genossenschaften. Vortrag, gehalten vor den
Genossenschaften Berlins am 19. März 1865. quotation of
Friedrich Thorwart (ed.): Hermann Schulze-Delitzsch's
Schriften und Reden. Vol. II Berlin 1909.

Schulze-Delitzsch, Hermann (1870): Erster Gesetzentwurf des
Verfassers. In: Die Entwickelung des Genossenschaftswesens
in Deutschland. Auszug aus dem Organ des Allgemeinen
Verbandes deutscher Erwerbs- und
Wirthschaftsgenossenschaften „Blätter für
Genossenschaftswesen" (früher Innung der Zukunft). Berlin.

Schulze-Delitzsch, Hermann (1876a): Protokolle der Sitzungen
des XVII. allgemeinen Vereinstages zu Danzig. In: Blätter für
Genossenschaftswesen (Innung der Zukunft XXIII. Jg.).

Schulze-Delitzsch, Hermann (1876b): Vorschuß- und Credit-
Vereine als Volksbanken. Praktische Anweisung zu deren
Errichtung und Gründung. 5th completely revised ed. Leipzig.

Schulze-Delitzsch, Hermann (1879): Jahresbericht für 1878 über die auf Selbsthilfe gegründeten Deutschen Erwerbs- und Wirthschaftsgenossenschaften. Leipzig.

Scirocco, Alfonso (1993): L'Italia del Risorgimento 1800 – 1871. New ed. Bologna.

Stappel, Michael (2015): Die deutschen Genossenschaften 2014. Entwicklungen – Meinungen – Zahlen. Wiesbaden.

Stein, Philipp (1928): Schulze-Delitzsch. In: Vahan Totomianz (ed.): Internationales Handwörterbuch des Genossenschaftswesens. Berlin.

Terberger, Thomas (2002): Der Mensch im Eiszeitalter. In: von Freden, Uta u. Siegmar Schnurbein: Spuren der Jahrtausende. Archäologie und Geschichte in Deutschland. Stuttgart.

Thüringer Waldgesetz(2015):http://landesrecht.thueringen.de/jportal/?quelle=jlink&query=WaldG+THGpsml=bsthueprod.psml&max=true. Consulted online on 01.11.2015.

Totomianz, Vahan (1928a): Russland und Sowjetunion. Das Genossenschaftswesen in Russland vor dem Kriege. In: Vahan Totomianz (ed.): Internationales Handwörterbuch des Genossenschaftswesens. Berlin.

Totomianz, Vahan (1928b): Owen. In: Vahan Totomianz (ed.): Internationales Handwörterbuch des Genossenschaftswesens. Berlin.

Totomianz, Vahan (1928c): King. In: Vahan Totomianz (ed.): Internationales Handwörterbuch des Genossenschaftswesens. Berlin.

Totomianz, Vahan (1928d): Byron. In: Vahan Totomianz (ed.): Internationales Handwörterbuch des Genossenschaftswesens. Berlin.

Totomianz, Vahan (1928e): Holyake. In: Vahan Totomianz (ed.): Internationales Handwörterbuch des Genossenschaftswesens. Berlin.

Totomianz, Vahan (1928f): Blanc. In: Vahan Totomianz (ed.): Internationales Handwörterbuch des Genossenschaftswesens. Berlin.

Totomianz, Vahan und A. Wingler (1928): Rochdaler Pioniere und ihre Taten. In: Vahan Totomianz (ed.): Internationales Handwörterbuch des Genossenschaftswesens. Berlin.

Ulitin, A. (1928): Artell. In: Vahan Totomianz (ed.):
Internationales Handwörterbuch des Genossenschaftswesens.
Berlin.

University of Michigan (2015):
http://www.umich.edu/~nasco/OrgHand/movement.html.
Consulted online on 29.09.2015.

Veiland-Haupt, Paul (1928): Dänemark. In: Vahan Totomianz
(ed.): Internationales Handwörterbuch des
Genossenschaftswesens. Berlin.

Venturini,Valentina (2011): Appunti sulle scritture teatrali. In:
Teatro e Storia on line; consulted online:
www.teatroestoria.it/doc/materiali/contrattoteatrali.
23.08.2015.

Weber, Karl-Wilhelm (1995): Alltag im Alten Rom. Zurich.

Weber, Max (1998): Die Kredit- und Agrarpolitik der preußischen
Landschaften. In: Gesamtausgabe Abt. I Schriften und Reden,
Vol. 8, Tübingen.

Wikipedia (2015):
https://de.wikipedia.org/wiki/Otto_von_Gierke. Consulted
online on 08.08.2015.

Wolf, Erik (1963): Große Rechtsdenker der deutschen
Geistesgeschichte. 4th revised and enhanced ed. Tübingen.

Wolff, Henry W. (1928): Großbritannien. Die
Genossenschaftsbewegung in Großbritannien. In: Vahan
Totomianz (ed.): Internationales Handwörterbuch des
Genossenschaftswesens. Berlin.

Wuttig, Adolf (1907): Friedrich Wilhelm Raiffeisen und die nach
ihm benannten ländlichen Darlehnskassen-Vereine. 5th ed.
Neuwied.

Wygodzinski, Willy (1911): Das Genossenschaftswesen in
Deutschland. Leipzig and Berlin.

Zawada, J. (1928): Polen. Die polnische
Genossenschaftsbewegung. In: Vahan Totomianz (ed.):
Internationales Handwörterbuch des Genossenschaftswesens.
Berlin.

Zeidler, Hugo (1893): Geschichte des deutschen
Genossenschaftswesens der Neuzeit. Leipzig.

Zschokke, Johann Heinrich (1918): Das Goldmacherdorf (Pioniere
und Theoretiker des Genossenschaftswesens, 1918, 2). Basel.

Also published by Wilhelm Kaltenborn

A forgotten past

The statutory obligation of all cooperatives to be affiliated to an auditing federation is a German speciality and is considered one of the reasons why there are relatively few cooperatives in Germany. Kaltenborn uses a wealth of material to prove that mandatory affiliation to auditing federations (Anschlusszwang), introduced with the amendment to the German Cooperative Societies Act in 1934, did not aim to enhance the economic resilience of cooperatives but was nothing more than the implementation of the National-Socialist Führerprinzip in the cooperative system.

Herausgeber: Heinrich-Kaufmann-Striftung
Verlag: Books on Demand GmbH
ISBN: 978-3-73-921503-7

Deutschsprachige Veröffentlichungen von Wilhelm Kaltenborn

Illusion und Wirklichkeit. Die Genossenschaftsidee: Fortwährender Begleiter der menschlichen Geschichte.

Auf deutschen Antrag hin soll die Genossenschaftsidee immaterielles UNESCO Kulturerbe werden. Tatsächlich begleiten Genossenschaften die Entwicklung und die Geschichte des Menschen von Anbeginn an und gehören deshalb unabhängig von allen Erklärungen der UNESCO so oder so zum immateriellen Weltkulturerbe.

Herausgeber: Zentralkonsum eG
Verlag: Books on Demand GmbH
ISBN: 978-3-7392-3227-0

Verdrängte Vergangenheit

Die Zwangsmitgliedschaft für Genossenschaften in einem Prüfungsverband wurde mit der Novelle zum Genossenschaftsgesetz im Jahr 1934 von Adolf Hitler zur Gleichschaltung und Eingliederung der Genossenschaften in die nationalsozialistische Zwangswirtschaft eingeführt. Kaltenborn belegt mit umfangreichem Material, dass der Zweck des Anschlusszwangs nicht die Stärkung der wirtschaftlichen Kraft der Genossenschaften, sondern die Durchsetzung des Führerprinzips des NS-Staates war.

Im Sinne der Gleichbehandlung mit anderen Rechtsformen und der Stärkung der Genossenschaften ist es an der Zeit, diese „deutsche Spezialität" ad acta zu legen und per Gesetz zu revidieren.

Herausgeber: Heinrich-Kaufmann-Stiftung
Verlag: Books on Demand GmbH
ISBN: 978-3-73-476148-5

Schein und Wirklichkeit

Kaltenborn zeichnet die Geschichte der Genossenschaftsverbände nach, untersucht, welchen Prinzipien die Verbände folgen sollten und wie sie tatsächlich mit ihren Mitgliedern, ihrer eigenen Geschichte, ihrem Erbe umgehen.

Er kommt zu dem Schluss, dass »Genossenschaftswesen« ein unbestimmter Begriff ist, der den Genossenschaftsgedanken in Deutschland eher vernebelt als erhellt, und er fordert die Verbände auf, sich weniger um die Rechtsform zu scheren, sondern im Sinne der Gründerväter um

Verlag: Das Neue Berlin Verlagsgesellschaft mbH
ISBN: 978-3-360-02189-2

Vision und Wirklichkeit

Kaltenborn hat in diversen er das Thema der genossenschaftlichen Herkunft und Wirklichkeit aus unterschiedlichen Blickwinkeln aufgearbeitet, um „die ursprünglichen Visionen ins Gedächtnis zu rufen, die die Genossenschaftsgründer einst geleitet haben".

Folgen Sie Wilhelm Kaltenborn auf den Spuren Hermann Schulze-Delitzschs und all derer, für die Genossenschaften gestern wie heute mehr sind als nur eine Rechtsform unter anderen.

Verlag: Das Neue Berlin Verlagsgesellschaft mbH
ISBN: 978-3-360-02152-6